CHARLES
FOUND AT LAST

CHARLES
FOUND AT LAST

A STORY OF THE ORPHAN TRAINS

DOROTHY URCH

Charles Found at Last: A Story of the Orphan Trains

Copyright 2023 by Dorothy M. Urch Estate

ISBN: 9781955295338

Courier Publishing
100 Manly Street
Greenville, SC 29601

Printed in the United States of America

Dedication

I wish to dedicate this book to the memory of my dear brother, Alfred Brooks Holmes, who was sent to Iowa as a two-year-old boy in 1904.

His heart was so broken because he thought his mother didn't love him.

I wish I had found out all of the information I now have and had helped him understand the reasons our mother decided it would be better for him to be placed in another home. I am sure she did what she thought was best for her children.

And so anyone who reads this and has also felt unloved or unwanted, God planned it so. His ways are best, and what we get is sometimes better than what we wanted in the first place.

Preface

My purpose in searching for facts is that I may show to my grandchildren and great-grandchildren the wonderful homes and parents they have, and how marvelous it is to have aunts, uncles, and cousins with whom they can have fellowship — not to mention the privilege of having grandparents to whom they can turn for examples and advice.

I also hope that they will preserve their own family history.

Not that I was deprived — far from it. I have three fathers — my birth father, Fred Brooks; my adoptive father, John Johnson; and my Heavenly Father, who adopted me in April of 1933.

I don't think there is any doubt that we (my family) are a part of American history, a part of the great placement of children with other families, which took place in America between the years of 1854 and 1929.

This search started when Pat Stewart, who taught a health class at Haywood Estates, a retirement home in Greenville, South Carolina, asked for a few facts about our lives. When I said that I had been born in New York, was sent to Iowa, and later adopted and lived there, she began to tell me about the "Orphan Trains," and the question was raised — could I have been one of those children who rode an Orphan Train?

Why was I put out for adoption? It could have been one or more reasons. My father died. There possibly were financial reverses, as I was told that at one time we had a lovely home, a maid, and all of the niceties of life. My mother also had health problems — a serious cardiac condition and inoperable hernias. I believe that two or three of my brothers were in the service during World War I, and, therefore, could not help. My oldest brother, Fred, told me he was in Paris when the Armistice was signed. He described how the people celebrated.

I am sure my mother loved us, and, as she did not want to put us in an orphanage, chose what she thought was the best alternative.

Why

Why God planned it so,
I probably will never know.
He sees the way that's hid from me,
The hills and valleys I cannot see.

I know I need not fret or fear,
To Him the path is plain and clear.
He knows the sorrows I must bear,
The joys that await me there.

He knows the strength from Him doth flow,
The patience I need to grow,
The time it takes to reach the goal,
The ups and downs to make me whole.

And so at last I'll be at rest.
The plan He had was much the best.
I'll understand His plan for me,
From worldly cares He'll set me free.

Written at 4 a.m., August 21, 1998
Buffalo Center, Iowa
Dorothy M. Urch

CHARLES

FOUND AT LAST

Department of Health   City of New York

BUREAU OF RECORDS

Certification of Birth

THIS IS TO CERTIFY that according to Birth Record No. _28282_ filed in the

Manhattan Office of the Bureau of Records on _June 8, 1911_

Dorothy Brook

Sex _Fem_ was Born in the City of New York, on _May 23, 1911_

In witness whereof, the seal of the Department of Health of the City of New York has

been affixed hereto this _6th_ day of _Sept_ 19_40_

John L. Rice, M.D.   _Thomas J. Duffield_   _John Nauran_

Commissioner of Health   Registrar of Records   Assistant Registrar of Records

Warning: This certification is not valid if it has been altered in any way whatsoever or if it does not bear the raised
seal of the Department of Health.

84-H-1938-2

Chapter I

Why?

I awoke with my chest still shaking and my eyes wet with tears. Why was I going to have to leave my dear Mamma (Mary Elizabeth) and ride for a long, long way on a big, noisy thing that they called a train? Why did I have to leave my beautiful home? Why did Mamma send brother William and brother Alfred to a place called Defiance, Iowa? Why did I have to leave all these people and houses and stores and go to live where you couldn't see another person or house? Then there would be all those strange animals — cows and horses and pigs and noisy chickens.

What would I do all day with no one to play with and my best friend and brother, Buddy, so far away?

Why did dear Papa have to die and be buried in a place call Kensico Cemetery?

Why wasn't there any money to buy food, and no one to help Mamma with the housework?

It was all such a mystery — too much for me to understand. Mamma loved me, wasn't that enough? I would be very good and do what I was told. My brothers, Buddy and Baby Charles, would be going to live somewhere else, too, and big brothers, Fred, Walter, and William, were far, far away doing something that was called "war."

Why had Grandfather Tyler gone back to England and didn't love Mamma anymore? The King of England thought he was a nice man and had given him some kind of honor.

What had happened to Papa's brothers, sisters, aunts and uncles in a place called San Francisco?

Mamma said I had two sisters whose names were Loretta and Beatrice, but they died before I was born, so I never got to see them.

Mamma came to my room to tell me that I needed to get up, get dressed, and eat some breakfast, as Miss Comstock was coming for Buddy and me pretty soon. The time had come for me to travel to my new home in Algona, Iowa.

I guess I should explain who Miss Comstock is. She is the lady who takes children to their new homes. Mamma says she is an agent for the New York Children's Aid Society, and she is a very nice, kind lady. Before taking the children away from their homes, she travels to different places. There she finds some good men who will see about the people who have said they would like to give children a new home. These people must promise to feed and clothe the children and send them to school and Sunday School. They must treat the children just like they would their own. They can also describe the kind of child they would like to have, and when Miss Comstock brings the children to their town, they can meet with the children and select one. My parents-

to-be, Mr. and Mrs. Johnson, had a little girl who died, and they wanted one to take her place.

Then Mamma explained to me again why she is sending me to live with some other people. There is no way she could leave us children alone while she worked, and there was very little chance she could get a job even if she had someone to care for us. Her health is very poor, too. Last night I heard her praying, and this is what she said:

Dear Father, I have come to you,
I simply don't know what to do.
My children need so many things,
Each day so many problems brings.

Their father's gone, I've done my part,
Dear Father, here's my broken heart.
Please give them homes with lots of love,
Their parent's wisdom from above.

Please teach them that I love them so.
There is no choice, they have to go.
Go with them, hold them in Thy care,
Help them to know You're always there.

Dear Father, heal my broken heart.
Watch over them as they depart.
Help them to know it's for the best.
Help them to turn to Thee for rest. Amen.

So I ran into her room and put my arms around her and said:

"Oh, Mamma dear, don't make me go."
"I'm sorry, dear, it's better so."
"I truly will be oh so good
And only do the things I should."

"It's not you, dear, you are just fine.
You've been so sweet, I'm glad you're mine.
But things have changed, it's different, so
I really have to let you go.

Things will be better, wait and see,
Or I wouldn't let you go from me.
You'll grow and change and then at last
You'll find these sad, sad days have passed."

She had told me, too, how she had sent my brothers William and Alfred, to Defiance, Iowa. My father had gone to San Francisco, California to find his family, but there had been a big earthquake and fire in San Francisco in 1907, and he could find no trace of them. He was gone so long that my mother thought he must be dead and was never coming back, so she had to find homes for them.

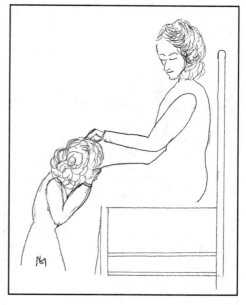

Then, after he died, she could not provide for us little ones — Albert, Charles, and me. But I didn't want to part with Charles, so I said, "Please, Mamma, could Charles go with Buddy and me? We could help take care of him. He is so little, he will be afraid of someone he doesn't know. They might not know what he eats, or how he likes to be rocked to sleep. Please, Mamma."

"Yes, Dorothy, I know you would take good care of him,

but Miss Hill has already found a Mr. and Mrs. Craig in Chanute, Kansas, who want a little boy like Charles. They have promised to take good care of him. There is no other way, honey. I must have an operation soon, and I have no one to take care of him. I don't have any money to hire someone, so I must do this."

"The reason we don't have any money," she said, "is that the man who was your father's business partner was not honest and made a lot of trouble for your father by cheating people. Your father felt bad about this and was determined to pay back all the money these people had lost. He worked so hard that he became ill and could no longer work. Do

you understand?"

"No, Mamma, I don't understand. I will go with Miss Comstock, but please come and get me soon," I answered.

When Miss Comstock came for us, Mamma, Buddy and I put on our coats, took Buddy's and my suitcases, and went to the New York Children's Aid Society. Some other boys and girls were there. "We must go now, children," said Miss Comstock. Mamma put her arms around me and we both cried. With one last look, she turned and left.

"All right, children, we must go now. Take your suitcase and follow me. We will go on the streetcar to Grand Central Station where the train is waiting."

Oh, how I wanted to say no, but Mamma had said I must be a good girl.

So we followed Miss Comstock, and in a little while we were at Grand Central Station.

Chapter II

The Trip West

We have arrived at the place where we will get on the train. It is called Grand Central Station, and it is a very big place, as there are trains going to many different places. The conductor tells us which car to get into, so Miss Comstock begins to carry the things to it that we are taking with us. We have all of our clothes, our food, and our emergency bag. After we are all on the train, we begin to put things away. I am frightened; I don't want to go, but Buddy says it is okay and that everything is going to be fine. Miss Comstock explains how we will do things. She says the first thing we will do is change our clothes, as she wants us to keep our new clothes nice, and we will put them on again when we stop at one of the places where we are going.

"When night comes, we will have to sleep sitting up," says Miss Comstock, "but that will be fun." I don't think it will be, but I guess we will be so tired we won't care.

The train is starting to pull out of the station now. It doesn't feel right to be someplace without Mamma. I hope I can come back soon. The buildings rush by so fast, and there aren't many houses to see now. Buddy says the big buildings

we can see now are factories. Clothes and furniture and all kinds of things are made in these buildings. Miss Comstock says that some of the big boys and girls work in those buildings. "I wish I could get a job," says Buddy, "and then we wouldn't have to leave New York."

Pretty soon there are no more buildings and we can see lots of trees. "Those are apple trees," explains Miss Comstock. "The reason they don't have any leaves on them is that the weather is too cold now. When the warm weather comes again, they will have beautiful pink flowers on them. Then the leaves will come and later on the lovely red apples. I wish we had one now. But let us change our clothes and put them away nicely. Then we will have a cookie and play a game or sing some songs."

The train is going faster now, and my head hurts. I want

to cry, but I am trying to be a brave girl. I know Mamma would want me to.

"What game would you like to play?" asks Miss Comstock, and when nobody says anything, she begins to sing. But nobody is very cheerful, and soon she stops. "Well, children, what would you like to do? Why don't we look out of the windows and talk about the things we see. A little while ago, I saw a river, and in the distance I can see some big hills. Tomorrow we will be in those big hills. They are really mountains, and they are called the Adirondack Mountains. These mountains have coal in them. Coal is a black, solid substance that is dug out of the ground and is used for fuel. Some of it we burn in our stoves to cook our food and keep us warm. Coal is burned in the engine that is pulling our train. It is used to make water very hot, and the steam from the water makes the power that makes the train move."

"What have you seen, Dorothy?"

"Oh, I saw a lot of water. What is that, Miss Comstock?"

"That is a lake. In a lake there are fish, which people catch and use for food. You can swim in a lake, too, or ride on it in a boat. When the weather gets very cold and stays that way for awhile, the water in the lake will freeze. Then sometimes large pieces of ice are just and taken into the city and used to help keep food cold. There are lots of things for us to learn about, and if you will ask me, I will try to tell you. It will be good for you to learn something about your new homes."

"Dorothy, a Mr. and Mrs. Johnson, who live on a farm, have asked for a little girl like you. I think it will be a fine place for you. They had one little girl, but she died, and since they cannot have more children, they will be glad to have you. I am sure they will love you," explained Miss Comstock. "Buddy, we will look for a good home for you when we get there. Would you like to live on a farm?"

"I would like to be a cowboy and fight Indians," replied Buddy.

But Miss Comstock said things are not like that anymore.

All of us are now hungry, so we unpack some sandwiches and some fruit and begin to eat. Miss Comstock explains that the train won't be stopping anyplace today, so we will eat some of what we brought along. After we finish eating, we will have some milk to drink. I am getting sleepy now, so Buddy lets me put my head in his lap. When I wake up, I can see the big hills getting closer. I turn to Miss Comstock and ask, "Miss Comstock, I wonder what Charles is doing."

"Oh, I think he is doing fine," replies Miss Comstock. "The lady, Miss Anna Hill, who is taking him to his new parents, is a very kind lady, and she will take good care of him. She will be sure that the people who are taking him are good to him." I don't say any more, but I wish I could have brought him with me.

"Before we get to the town of Lewisburg, Pennsylvania, where John is going to a new home, let me tell you about the

New York Children's Aid Society," says Miss Comstock. "It was started by a man by the name of Charles Loring Brace. He had studied to be a preacher, but when he saw so many children on the street of New York who were sleeping on the streets and stealing food or eating from garbage cans, he decided to do something about it. So he got some men to help. They rented a big building, got some beds, food, and clothing, and took some children there. Then he sent people to different places to find new homes for them. He believed that children would grow up to be good people if they had good food, plenty of fresh air, good surroundings, and good examples. I believe that, too. John, your new parents live in a small town. Your new father works in a factory. He loves boys, and as his three boys are almost grown, he wants another little boy to raise. His name is John, too! I will come back to visit you soon. I'm sure you will be happy in your new home."

"You weren't on the streets, Dorothy, but your mother is not well and couldn't get a job so she could take care of you and Buddy and Charles. That is why she decided to find new homes for you. I am sure she loved you very much and did what she thought was best. She didn't have any family here in the United States, and your father's family all perished in the big earthquake and fire in San Francisco, California. You see, it isn't that people wanted to send their children away; there were just lots of things that happened that they couldn't do anything about, so they did what they thought was best."

"We need to eat some lunch now, children, and then we will change our clothes and make ourselves neat. We want the people where we stop to see we are a nice group."

So we eat our lunch and make ourselves look nice. Soon the train begins to slow down and finally stops. We all climb down from the train and begin to look around. John says, "I wonder which man will be my new father." Miss Comstock is talking to a nice-looking man and lady, and soon she calls John to come and meet his new father and mother.

"Oh, I hope John likes them and is happy," I think to myself.

Some other people are talking to Miss Comstock, too, and some of them are talking to some of the children. I take Buddy's hand and say, "Let's go for a walk. I'm frightened, and I don't want to talk to anybody." So Buddy and I walk a little way and look at the town. Soon we hear Miss Comstock calling us to come back and get on the train, as we must go on, and it will soon be night.

When we get back on the train, we change our clothes and get ready for bed. But there are not beds, so we will sleep sitting up. Some of the children are getting very cross, so Miss Comstock tells us to say our prayers, and then she will sing us a song. Oh, how I wish I were at home in my own bed. Maybe things will be better in the morning.

"What is that bright light, Buddy?" I ask.

"That's the sun, Dorothy. It's time to wake up."

I look around. Where am I? Oh, yes, I remember now. We are on a train, going to a new place. "Good morning, children," says Miss Comstock pleasantly. "Let's wash our hands and faces, and then we will have an orange and some bread and jelly. We have some cans of milk to drink when you have finished eating."

The train is going rather slowly now, and we seem to be going around a hill and up and down. Buddy says we are now in the Pocono Mountains. I don't like it very much, but he says we will soon be past them.

Before long we are riding through open country. I can see some big buildings and some tall things. Miss Comstock says these are "barns" and "silos." The barns are for the cows to stay in and the silos have feed stored in them to feed the cows during the winter. "The people who live in this part of Pennsylvania are farmers," explains Miss Comstock, "and they will be happy to have some strong, healthy boys to help. They are hardworking people, but they are very kind and their wives are excellent cooks. Any boy who gets to live here is very fortunate."

"Before we stop again, and some more of you go to your new homes," Miss Comstock says, "I want to tell you about your birth parents. They are good people, and they love you very much. The reason they are sending you away is that they can no longer give you good homes. So many people have come to New York from other countries that there are no longer enough jobs for everybody."

"Kathleen, she says, "your grandparents came from Ireland because the potato crops had failed for several years, and there was not enough food in Ireland."

"Abe," Miss Comstock continues, "your family left Germany because the leaders there did not like Jewish people, and they were afraid for their lives. None of you children lived on the streets as many boys and girls did, but your parents brought you to the New York Children's Aid Society. So many boys and girls came there, we had to find another way to care for everyone. This is why I am taking you to new homes."

"Well," she then said, "we must get ready now to meet some of these people. See, our train is slowing down, and we are pulling into the station. At this place there is a man and lady who have asked for a nice girl to help care for a baby, as the lady is not very well. I think you will love these people, Kathleen, and they will have a good older sister for their baby."

"Dorothy and Buddy," Miss Comstock told us, "I will tell you about your birth parents when you get back on the train."

So, again we alight from the train to find a crowd of people waiting for us. I don't like it very well — these people staring at us — but Miss Comstock moves briskly among them, smiling and shaking hands. Finally, she comes back and takes Kathleen to see a young couple. I can see that the lady is carrying a small baby. Kathleen begins to smile, and

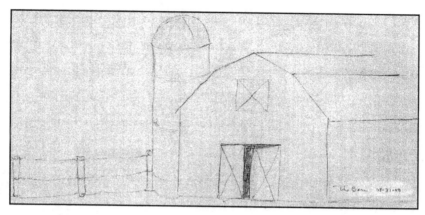

soon she is holding the baby. I guess she will like her new home, and I am glad.

After we get back on the train, we change our clothes again We put them back in our suitcases, and Miss Comstock gives us a cookie.

"Let me tell you about your birth parents," says Miss Comstock. "Dorothy and Buddy, your father and mother were fine people. Your mother was born in New Jersey. After her mother died, her father went back to England. He must have been a very stern man, so your mother decided to stay in this country. Your father was born in San Francisco. His family all perished or were lost in the San Francisco 1907 earthquake and fire. That meant that you had no grandparents, aunts, or uncles left to help care for you. Your father's business partner ruined their business. Then your father got sick and died. Your mother had no one to help care for you. Your big brothers were in Europe fighting in the war."

"Children, I hope you understand your mothers are not sending you away because they don't love you. They love you very much. They don't want you to live in an orphanage. They want you to live where you can have both mother and father, where there is plenty to eat and fresh air and sunshine. Mr. Brace, who is the head of the New York Children's Aid Society feels the same way. He wants what is best for you."

"Thank you, Miss Comstock," we say. "Do you think our mothers will come and get us?"

"I can't tell you that for sure," replies Miss Comstock, "but I know you have good homes waiting for you. I hope you will do your best to love and obey the people who are giving you homes."

Again our train is moving fast, and we can no longer see the mountains. "Emily, your new home will be near Akron, Ohio," Miss Comstock explains. "You will be living with a widow lady. She lives on a farm, but she has people to do the work. She needs someone to keep her company. She is a very pretty lady who does good things for other people. I know you will love her. A twelve-year-old girl like you can be a big help at making other people happy. Frank and Susan, your new homes are in Indiana. You will be living in different homes, but you will go to the same school and church. You will see each other often. Your new parents, Frank, live on a dairy farm. They have lots of cows to milk, so you'll probably help with that. Susan's home is in a small village. Her father owns the blacksmith shop and her mother is the postmistress. You can write me a letter often,

Susan," laughs Miss Comstock. "Now I think we had better have something to eat and try to get some sleep. Tomorrow will be another long day."

So another night passes, and the train is taking me farther and farther away from my mother. Oh, what will happen? Will I ever see her again? And Baby Charles-does he cry for Mamma? I still don't understand why these things had to happen. I'm so glad Buddy is with me.

"Today," explains Miss Comstock, "we will leave Bob in Elgin, Illinois. We will be changing trains in Chicago first. This train doesn't go all the way to Algona, Iowa. Bob, you will live on a farm where lots and lots of corn is grown. This corn is used to feed many pigs that are raised there. I am sure you will have many good things to eat. During the winter, some of the pigs are butchered. Pig meat is made into ham, bacon, pork chops and pork roasts. Lard is used to fry food and to make the crust for all kinds of good pies. I expect you will be as fat as a pig the next time I see you," laughs Miss Comstock.

Pretty soon we change our clothes for our next stop which is Chicago. We gather up all our things and pack them away so that we can take them with us on the next train. When the train stops, the conductor helps us, and together we go to the next train, which will take us to Iowa. Oh, I will be so glad when this long ride is over. We can't really get clean as the train belches out black smoke and soot. The seats are so hard that we can't be comfortable, and of course, we have not been able to lie down to sleep these past three nights. Our sandwiches are dry too, and the fruit is beginning to spoil. "Mamma, please come to get me," I whisper.

Now we are on the train again. Before long, Miss Comstock has Bob get his things together, and soon we are in Elgin. Miss Comstock tells Emily, Buddy, and me to stay on the train. Soon she is back again. When we stop again, Bob leaves with his new parents. We are now nearing the Mississippi River where we cross into Iowa. By night we reach the river and cross it on a big bridge. Then Miss Comstock tells us she wants us to get some sleep. I am so tired.

Sometime during the night the train stops at Mason City, and Martha's new parents take her home with them. I am too sleepy to really know about that. When the train stops again, Miss Comstock says, "Here we are, Buddy and Dorothy." We are finally in Algona, Iowa!

Chapter III

The Arrival

At last we are in Algona. Our long ride is over, and I am very tired. After getting off the train, we will go to the hotel, where we will have breakfast and have a bath and a nap. After lunch we will change into our best clothes and go to the Call Opera House where we will meet our new parents. What will mine look like? Will they be kind people? Will they like the way I look? What will we say to each other?

We sit on a stage with the people in front of us who want children. Miss Comstock explains the reason we are there and what our new parents will promise to do for us. Then the committee of local people, who have planned all this, will explain to the people who want us (and to us) what we are to do.

The people who want children must have described what they wanted, and they seem to know which child they want. Now a nice-looking couple is coming toward me, and Miss Comstock says, "Mr. and Mrs. Johnson, this is Dorothy. I think I have brought you a little girl who will suit you just fine. She is five years old and has blue eyes and blond hair, as you requested. She has nice manners and is very well behaved. I know you will love her and take good care of her. If you will please sign this contract, I will see what I can do about her brother."

"Oh, Miss Comstock, don't make me leave Buddy. I want to do what you tell me to do, but I want my Mamma and my brother."

"Yes, dear, I understand, but if you will just go with Mr. and Mrs. Johnson

The Johnsons

now, I will come to see you tomorrow, and we will talk about this some more. Buddy is going to stay in Algona with Mrs. Rawson, and you will get to see him real often. There will be lots of new things for you to see and do. You will have lots of good things to eat and a nice bed to sleep in."

So I tell Buddy, "Good-bye," and Mrs. Johnson takes my hand.

"Let's go home, Dorothy," she says. But I am afraid of Mr. Johnson, as he hasn't shaved, and his whiskers are long. He looks kind, though, so I take Mrs. Johnson's hand, and we start for the door. A pretty lady with beautiful white hair stands up, and Mrs. Johnson says, "This is my mother, Dorothy. She will be your grandmother now." A grandmother.

That will be nice. I had never known a grandmother, as my Mamma's mother died a long time ago, and my father's mother is dead, too.

Now we are out of doors and walking towards a big wagon. "This is the way we will go home," explains Mrs.

County Advance

IOWA, WEDNESDAY, FEBRUARY 28, 1917   NUMBER 3

HOME IN KOSSUTH WANTED FOR BOY NINE YEARS OLD

Another Homeless New York Orphan is Brought to Algona.

LITTLE SISTER HAS BEEN
       TAKEN BY LOCAL FARMERS

Brother Is Bright, Happy Child and is at Present at the Home of Mrs. Rawson, of Algona.

Wanted-Good home for nice little boy of nine, of good American parentage. Bright, healthy, and well mannered. May be seen at Mrs. E.J. Rawson's, 202 east Call street, Algona.

This little want "ad" was left with the Advance Thursday by Miss Clara B. Comstock, one of the two representatives of the Children's Aid Society, of New York. Who found good homes here a year ago for 14 homeless New York boys and girls.

Miss Comstock brought the boy here last Wednesday, but, being pressed for time, had to postpone looking up a home for him. Mrs. Rawson heard of the case, and volunteered to open her home and big, motherly heart to the youngster until a place was found for him.

The boy's little sister, aged 5, has been placed with Mr. and Mrs. J.A. Johnson, six miles southeast of Algona. Mr. and Mrs. Johnson have no other children.

Miss Comstock left here for Charles City, where, on Friday, she and her able coadjutor, Miss Anna Hill, were to find homes for 12 children from New York. Miss Hill is the young woman of somewhat ample proportions who made such an excellent impression upon a crowded house at the Call when she appealed for homes for the children who were brought here a year ago.

After disposing of the children taken to Charles City, Miss Comstock will come back to Algona and find a home for the boy at Mrs. Rawson's

Miss Comstock said that the children brought here last year were all still in the county. A few, however, have been changed to other homes for one reason or another. All are doing well, and none of the foster parents has had reason to regret having taken one or more of the children.

Persons desirous of corresponding with Miss Comsotck relative to the boy at Mrs. Rawson's may address her at Des Moines, P.O. Box No. 117.

Clara B. Comstock, Western Agent for the Children's Aid Society. Photo anbd information courtesy of the New York Children's Aid Society and Ethel Lambert.

Johnson. "You see, the roads are so muddy now after the snow has melted that we would get stuck if we came in the car." Oh my, what a funny way to live, I thought. Aren't there any streets? And I don't think I'm going to like riding in that wagon behind those big horses. Mr. Johnson helps us into the wagon, and we start for home. Again I am surprised that there are so few houses. Mrs. Johnson explains that the other big buildings are barns and that is where the animals live. After what seems a long time, we stop at a house, and Mrs. Johnson says this will be my new home.

The house is small, and when we go inside, I see that there are only two rooms, but there are two more upstairs. While we take off our coats and hang them behind the door, Mr. Johnson puts the horses in the barn. It is beginning to get dark now, so Mrs. Johnson goes to a big black thing, opens the top and puts some wood in it. This is the stove, and it is to keep us warm and cook our food. Her mother helps her; they put some food in pans and put them on the stove. The food smells good, and I am hungry, as we didn't have any hot food on the train. When Mr. Johnson comes in, he washes his hands, but there is no sink so he puts some water in a pan and washes his hands in it. My, this is a funny house!

Before we can eat, Mrs. Johnson lights a lamp. Where I used to live we had electric lights. The lamp doesn't give much light, but it does seem kind of homey, and the food is good. When we finish eating, Mr. Johnson goes out to the barn to take care of the animals for the night. When Mrs. Johnson and her mother finish washing the dishes, Mrs. Johnson says, "I think you had better get ready for bed, Dorothy. You have had a long trip, and I am sure you are tired." She picked up the lamp, took my hand, and we went upstairs. Oh, I am so tired,-so when I have put on my night-gown, I say my prayers. "Dear Father, I don't understand all of this. Why did I have to leave my Mamma? And Baby Charles — he is so little, dear God. I'll try to be a good girl and obey my new mamma and papa."

"It's all so strange. I don't know why my dearest Papa had to die. I had to leave my Mamma dear to live with these new people here. And Baby Charles, he needs your love. Watch over him from up above. Amen."

"Dear Dorothy, please don't be so sad. We want you to be happy. You see, our little girl went to be with Jesus, and we wanted another little girl so we chose you. We already love you, and we want you to call us Mamma and Papa," explained Mrs. Johnson. "Some day I will show you where she is buried, and you can put flowers on her grave. Her name was Clara Mae. Why don't you get in bed and let me cover you up. I will stay with you until you go to sleep. If you need any- thing in the night, Papa

and I will be in the next room, and your new grandmother will come and sleep with you." So I closed my eyes and soon I was asleep.

The next morning when I woke up, I didn't know where I was for a little while. Something really smelled good, and I was hungry, so I went downstairs. "Good morning, Doro- thy. I hope you slept well," said my new Mamma.

"Yes, I did, and I am hungry, but where do I take my bath?"

Mamma laughed. "Just come and eat your breakfast, and I will explain your new life on a farm," she replied.

When I had finished my breakfast, we went upstairs so I could dress. "You see, Dorothy, we don't have a bathtub here in our little house, so we have to wash as best we can. On the stove in the kitchen, we have what we call a reser- voir. We fill it with cold water and it gets hot. We use some of that water to make the cold water warm enough to wash ourselves with. We also use some of the water to wash our dishes and pans. Papa has to start a gasoline motor to pump the water from the well. Then he carries it to the house. He puts some water in a pail, too, so that we may have water to drink. When I need to wash clothes, we fill a big container, heat the water on the stove, and then put the water in a tub with some soap. When we have rubbed the clothes clean, we wring the water out of them and put them in another tub of clean water to rinse. In the summertime, I hang the clothes on a clothesline outdoors to dry. After we have finished washing the clothes, we carry the dirty water outside and throw it away. When we build our new house, we won't have to carry water, and we will have a drain to take all of the dirty water away."

"Now we need to get ready for Miss Comstock to come to see you," she said. "We want everything to look nice so that she will be pleased with your new home."

Chapter IV

My First Day at School

Mamma and Papa bought me a tablet, some pencils, and a box of Crayolas to take to school.

My teacher's name is Grace Johnson, and she is a very nice lady.

This is what we do. First, we say the "Pledge of Allegiance": "I pledge allegiance to the flag of the United States of America and to the Republic for which it stands."

I don't know what all that stands for, but it sounds very nice. We have to stand and put our right hand over our heart. Then we sing "America" and "The Star Spangled Banner." We don't have a piano, but Miss Johnson has a nice voice, and we all enjoy singing. Then Miss Johnson reads us a story. I enjoy that so much and will be so happy when I can read.

The inside of the schoolhouse is very nice. There are several rows of seats. Miss Johnson showed me mine. It is small so I can sit with my feet on the floor. The seats for the big boys and girls are larger.

Miss Johnson's desk is on a platform in the front of the room. Behind her desk are two big blackboards and a big

map, which can be pulled down to see it or rolled up so that you can't see it. There are windows on both sides of the room and some pictures on the walls. One is a picture of George Washington and the other of Abraham Lincoln. Miss Johnson says they were presidents of our country and that I will learn more about them later.

On a shelf in the back of the room is a wash pan so that we can wash our hands. Beside it is a pail of water and a dipper so we can get a drink.

"Today, Dorothy, you may listen and watch. Tomorrow I will show you how to print your name, and when Florence comes up on the platform, you may come with her, and we will begin to learn some letters and later learn to read," explains Miss Johnson. "This is called Phonics. We learn both the name and the sound of each letter. When we have learned to do that, we will put the letters together to make words." (I can hardly wait.) "You may take out your paper and Crayolas and make a picture if you want."

So I do that, and pretty soon Miss Johnson says it is recess time. So we put our things away and put on our coats, as it is still cold outside. We also have to put on our boots, as there is snow on the ground. When I dressed this morning, Mamma made me put on some long underwear, some long stockings, a pair of bloomers, and a flannel petticoat under my dress. It seemed like a lot of clothes, but Mamma explained that the schoolhouse might be cold as the stove was in the middle of the room and my desk might not be near it. "We don't want you to be cold or get sick," said Mamma. "You are so new here, and we wouldn't want Miss Comstock to think we aren't taking good care of you." After breakfast I put on something she called "leggings." They were pieces of cloth which wrapped around my legs and buttoned up the side. I thought I looked funny, but the other girls had on that kind of clothes, too.

When we go out of doors, there were some big piles of snow. Florence explained to me that they were called "snowdrifts" and were made by the wind blowing the snow into piles. Some of the big boys got a shovel and begin to dig tunnels in them. It was fun, but recess was soon over, and we had to go back into the schoolhouse.

I was beginning to get tired when Miss Johnson told us to put our things away and get ready for lunch. I am going home at noon and won't come back this afternoon. Mamma thought I should start out a little slowly after my long trip and all. I like school and will be glad when I can go all day.

Let me tell you some more about my new school. It is a long wood building. It is painted white. It has a belfry with a big bell in it. When it is time for school to begin, the teacher rings the bell. Sometimes, as a special privilege, one of the children is allowed to ring it.

There are two buildings in back of the schoolhouse. One is marked "Girls" and the other is marked "Boys." That's where we go for the "necessaries." Beside the schoolhouse is another small building where coal and cobs are kept. (Do you know what cobs are? That's what corn grows on. After the corn is shelled, the cobs are used for fuel.) In the winter, the teacher must keep a fire in the big stove so that the children will be warm.

Out in the yard there is a flag pole. Every day when the weather is nice, the United States flag is displayed. It makes me to proud to see it fluttering in the breeze.

There is a swing and a teeter-totter to play with outdoors when the weather is nice. We also have a bat and a ball. When the weather is cold, we play games like "Button, Button, Who's Got the Button?" and other games indoors. We do this during recess and noon. Sometimes the teacher

will read us a story. I really like that. I will be so happy when I can read. We have a big bookcase in the back of the room. There are some nice books in it. Mamma will get me some books of my own, too. She says I will like the one by a man named Robert Louis Stevenson. There is poem in it about a swing. I had never had a swing, but Papa said he will make me one when the weather gets warm. Did you know you can make a swing out of an old tire? You can also make one out of a bag filled with sand. I think I am going to like living in the country.

Miss Johnson had to scold some girls this morning. They were doing too much giggling when they should have been studying. I am going to try to be good 'cause Miss Johnson can punish us if we do something wrong. I know Papa and Mamma would feel bad. They probably would scold me, too. Then, too, I told my real Mamma and Miss Comstock that I would be a good girl. We should keep our promises, shouldn't we?

When we are thirsty we can get a drink from the pail of water in the back of the room. Two of the big boys carry the water from my house. There is only one dipper, so we all drink from it. I guess that is okay.

I wonder if Buddy went to school today. He is staying in town with Mrs Rawson, so he will go to a big school. Charles is too little to go to school. I hope his new mamma is taking good care of him.

Florence said that sometimes we have a program at night. Our parents come to hear us speak and sing songs. Miss Johnson will light the lamps that are fastened to the wall. They are filled with something called kerosene. One end of a wick is in the kerosene and that is what burns and makes the light. Such strange things!

I know I will be frightened to speak, but maybe I can say:

I know two magic little words
That make a way for me.
The first is "Thank you."
Next is "Please" — just you wait and see.

We might all sing the "The Star Spangled Banner" or "America." Sometimes some of the boys and girls do a play. They get to dress up in different clothes. Miss Johnson hangs some sheets in front of the platform to make a stage. Florence also told me about something she called a "box social."

The ladies fix a pretty box and fill it with good things to eat. The man that will pay the most for that box gets it and gets to eat with the lady who made it. When the boxes are sold, the money is given to the school. It is used to buy books for the library, a picture, or maybe a new flag. That sounds like fun. I guess the people who live in the country do more things together than we did in New York.

There is a lot more I could tell you about my school and my new life. I guess there will be plenty of time. I hope Mamma will come for me soon, but if she can't, I will try to do my best and make her proud of me.

Miss Comstock is coming to see me tomorrow. If my new parents have decided to keep me, she will leave and come back later.

I have been with my new parents for two weeks now. Miss Comstock is pleased that things are going so well. My home will now be on the farm, and I will be going to school here for eight years. Buddy thinks my school is very odd — he goes to a big school in town. All the boys and girls in his room are in the same grade. I wonder what kind of school Charles will go to.

Let me tell you more about my school.

When the weather gets warm, we will play out of doors at recess and at noon. Florence told me that sometimes the boys catch a snake and chase the girls with it. Aren't boys awful? I've never seen a snake, and I don't think I'm going to like them very much. It will be fun to have a big yard to play in. The houses in New York are so close together that there isn't much room for a yard. We have to go to a park to play on swings and teeter-totters.

Some of the children here have a long way to walk to school. The bigger ones have chores to do after school. No one likes to stay after school for punishment if they have done something wrong. That usually results in more trouble at home as parents believe in the teacher's good judgment and may add a little more punishment.

Today was cold, so Miss Johnson put some more cobs in the stove. She put in too many at once, and soon we had to open the windows to let out the smoke. When the weather gets warm, we will open the windows to keep us cool.

Mamma and Papa are very good to me, and Mamma is teaching me many things. Today Papa and a neighbor will butcher a pig. This is done so we can have meat to eat. After the pig has been killed, dipped in boiling water, and the hair scraped off, it is hung out-of-doors until morning. It is then taken to the house to be cut into pork chops and pork roasts. Some of the meat is ground and made into sausage. The fat part is cooked in the oven and drained — this becomes lard. Part of the meat is cooked and put into jars for later use. Mamma salts part to keep it longer.

There are so many things I can learn on a farm. Farmers do many things for themselves — make butter, grow their own vegetables, and even have fruit trees. Mamma calls this being "self-sufficient." Boys who live on farms learn to care for the animals, repair the machinery, and harvest the crops. Buddy would like to live on a farm.

I have learned to print my name now, to count to twenty, and say some of my ABCs. "You are a good girl, and you are learning fast," says Mamma. "We are very proud of you." When I say my prayers at night, I thank God for my new home.

Chapter V

Early Childhood

I'm in the third grade now, and I have the nicest teacher. Her name is Ruth Lindsay, and she has the prettiest hair. Do you know what she asked me today? Would I like to go home with her after school and stay all night? Of course, we have to ask my Mamma if I can, but I am so excited! We will walk a mile and a half, get on the train, and go to her house. She lives in town. None of the other boys and girls have done this, and I am very proud to be chosen.

Today Mamma got a letter from Miss Comstock, and we talked about her. I don't really remember much about her. Mr. and Mrs. Johnson seem like my own "Papa" and "Mamma," and New York and other people seem like a dream. With all my new friends, school, and all the things I have to do, some things are not very real. I can't remember what Charles looked like, and I am not sure how old he is. I wonder if he is happy and if his parents are as good to him as my Mamma and Papa are to me.

Mamma is making me a beautiful new dress. She is making it from her twin sister's wedding dress. It is so shiny and beautiful. I am to have some white stockings, some new white shoes, and a big white hair bow to wear with it. Oh, I will feel so elegant. I am going to have my picture taken, too. Maybe I can send one to Miss Comstock. I wrote her a letter — she was so pleased.

Buddy spent Saturday and Sunday with me. He isn't very happy. Mrs. Rawson makes him wash dishes and sweep the floors. (She has a rooming-boarding house.) She doesn't let him go to play with his friends very often. He wishes he

Dorothy's new dress (age 7)

could go back to New York, but our birth mother still can't take care of him. He isn't old enough to get much of a job either. My Mamma and Papa love him, but they don't want to raise a boy, too. The people who adopted Charles moved to Canada, so we don't hear about him anymore. I guess this is best — we all have plenty to eat, a good place to live, and good clothes to wear. Sometimes some of the boys and girls tease me about being adopted. I don't care. I tell them, "My Mamma and Papa chose me. Yours had to take what they got."

Florence and I got scolded in school today. We sit in

a double seat, and sometimes things get so funny we can't stop laughing.

Last night we went to visit our neighbors. They have two girls, Marguerite and Roberta. Their mother made a big pan of popcorn for us. We took it into the living room to eat. We told each other ghost stories. We didn't have any lights on, so it was really scary.

I can read now, so sometimes Mamma lets me take an apple, a bowl of popcorn, and a book to bed with me. I think that is one of my most favorite things.

I like to play with my doll and doll carriage, too. She is such a pretty doll. Her head and hands are made of china, so I have to treat her very gently. Mamma makes her lots of pretty clothes.

Today we had a spelling bee at school. I won a prize for spelling "alphabet" correctly. Reading and spelling are my favorite subjects.

We have lots of fun times at school. I like to play "Ante I Over" and "Pom-Pom-Pull-Away." Our teacher plays with us sometimes. She is a good teacher and a good example. She always grades us fairly and explains things to us if something is wrong.

Mamma teaches me many good things, too. I have some chores to do — Mamma and Papa think that children need to do a little work. Mamma says, "The devil will find work for idle hands to do." I don't always understand what my teacher and parents say, but I know that they have learned these things. I guess "Experience is the best teacher."

One of my chores is to take leftover food to a cool place. We don't have an icebox or refrigerator. Back of our house is a building that we call a "storm cave." It has a cellar that is cool even on hot days. Mamma keeps her canned food there, too. In the summer when there is extra food in the garden, she cooks the vegetables and puts them in glass jars. That gives us good things to eat all winter. The storm cave is used for another thing, too. When Papa sees bad looking clouds or when the wind blows hard, we go there for safety. The building is made of big rocks cemented together. It is not very tall, and it has a flat roof made of cement. Sometimes there are bad tornadoes in Iowa. The storm cave helps to keep us safe.

After Papa has milked the cow, we put the milk in the cave to cool. When it has cooled and the cream comes to the

top, Mamma skims it off and puts it in a big bowl she calls a "crock." When the cream has soured and she has a bowl full, she churns it into butter. The churn is a big container. A wooden handle with four cross pieces on the bottom is moved up and

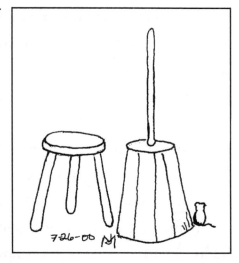

down in the churn until the butter forms. The liquid that is left is good to drink. Mamma makes the butter into big patties. We take butter and eggs to the grocery store and trade them for sugar, flour, coffee, and tea.

In the winter, we usually go to town in a big sled. Two horses, named King and Queen, pull the sled. In the summer, we go in the car. It is a Saxon and is called a touring car. It doesn't have windows. When it rains, we fasten some sheets of canvas to the top and to the car. There are little windows in the canvas so that we can see out. They are made of "isinglass" or mica. Our roads are covered with gravel, which makes them very dusty when it is dry. The cars don't go very fast anyway — I guess about forty miles an hour. The wheels have wood spokes in them, and sometimes they get broken.

Another of my jobs is to help feed the chickens. I like to do that. In warm weather, the chickens are outdoors all day.

They are such busy little creatures, looking and scratching the ground for bugs and worms. We feed them corn and other things. We just scatter the feed on the ground, and they pick it up. We feed the dog with leftover food from the table. Papa gives the cats warm milk when he milks the cow. They live in the barn and catch the mice. That is very helpful, as the mice eat the corn that we need to feed the chickens and pigs.

I am going to have a busy summer watching some men build our new house. First, they will dig a basement and finish it with blocks and cement for the walls and floor. The first floor will have a kitchen, dining room, and living room.

Upstairs there will be three bedrooms and a bathroom. There will be a big attic, too, and a nice front porch. I will have my own room. I get to choose the color I want the walls painted and some new curtains. I am so excited!

Tomorrow is the first day of May. We are going to make May baskets. I have some colored construction paper that I will fold, cut, and paste together to make the baskets. Then I will fill them with homemade candy, popcorn, or some violets. Some of these pretty little purple flowers are growing in our yard. We will take the baskets to people who are shut-ins.

I will take them to the door, knock on the door, and run away before they can thank me. Mamma is teaching me to be kind to sick or elderly people. She is very strict with me about my manners. She says, "Handsome is as handsome does." That means that being polite and kind is more important than being pretty. She wants me to be a lady. I don't wear slacks so she tells me to keep my feet and skirts down. The trouble is: I like to hang upside down from a tree limb. There is such a nice one in our backyard.

School will soon be out for vacation. We will have lots of things to do. The garden is growing nicely, but we need to keep the weeds pulled or the vegetables will not do well. Everything is so good fresh from the garden. Mamma shows me how to know when the vegetables are ready to eat. There

is always something to learn when you live on a farm. When Mamma and I work in the garden, we wear a sunbonnet to shade our face. A sunbonnet is made of a round piece of cloth with another piece of cloth sewed on the front. We tie it under our chins. Mine is pink. It is so pretty.

I was really frightened yesterday when a strange man knocked on our door and asked for something to eat. His clothes were sort of ragged, and he didn't look too clean. Mamma told him she would give him some food if he would chop some wood. Then she explained to me that some men who don't have jobs go from place to place and will work for food. These men ride in the boxcars on the trains. They sleep wherever they can. They are called "tramps" or "hobos." That's almost like some children had to do in New York. Wasn't my birth mother wise in sending me to Iowa? I'll never have to do that.

My birthday is May 23, and Mamma is planning a birthday party for me. I will invite Florence, Lucille, Roberta, and Mildred. I am to have a cake with pink frosting. Oh, boy! I guess I will be getting a new book. I like that.

Life on a farm is so interesting. In the city where I lived, there are lots of big buildings. There is a park we could go to, but it wasn't very big. Many people went there, too. I still miss my birth mother and my brothers, but I have a wonderful home.

Last winter, Mamma taught me how to sew. We cut out little pieces of cloth. Then we sewed different colors and patterns together in long rows. When we had the rows sewed together, we laid the pieces on a big sheet of cotton. Next, we laid them both on a big piece of plain cloth and tied yarn in the corners. After that, we sewed around the edges. That made a nice quilt that we use to keep us warm. Mamma knows how to crochet and embroider. She will teach me as I get older. We never waste anything. Mamma says, "Waste not, want not." When our clothes get worn spots in them, we cut out the good parts and tear them into strips. We sew these strips into long pieces and then crochet or braid them to make rugs. They are very pretty.

In the evening we read or play games. I like to play "Cat's Cradle." A long piece of string is tied together, and one player puts it on a finger of each hand and stretches it out. Then the second player takes two pieces between her thumbs and forefingers. The string is then changed to her hands. By going back and forth in this manner, the string takes 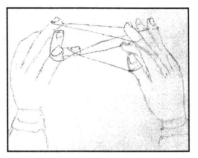 on different shapes, one of which looks like a cradle. Making shadow pictures on the wall by lamplight is fun, too. Of course, you have to use your imagination, which is good for me to do.

Papa is busy in the winter, too. He repairs anything that is broken on the farm machinery. Then he cleans and oils the plows, harrows, discs, and the corn planter. He sharpens the ax, the saw, and the hoes. He cuts and splits wood that we use to cook our food and keep us warm. The harness that the horses wear to pull the sled and machinery is repaired and oiled. A good farmer takes good care of his ma-

chinery and his buildings as well as his animals. Sometimes if it isn't too cold, Papa repairs fences and broken places in the barn and other farm buildings. He also cleans the hog house and makes new pens for the baby pigs that will be born in March. (They are so cute and fat. They want to eat all the time, and they are noisy little creatures.) Papa checks to see if he has plenty of seed to plant and orders more if he needs it.

When April comes, Mamma is busy putting eggs in a big box called an "incubator." There is a small lamp in it to keep the eggs warm. The eggs must be turned every day. In three weeks, the baby chickens will hatch. I like to watch.

First, you can see a tiny crack in the egg. Then small pieces start to break off, and soon you can see a little bill and two little eyes. Before long, the baby chick breaks the shell

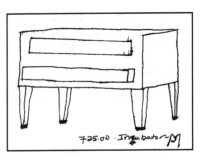

$25.00 · Incubator

and comes out. At first it is a little wobbly, and it looks like it might be wet. But soon it gets nice and fluffy and begins to move around. What a noise there is as, one after another, the baby chicks emerge from their shells. Such a "peep-peep" you have never heard!

When all the chickens have hatched, they are put into

a little building called a "brooder" house. In this building there is a small heater to keep them warm. We also put pans of water and feed in the building for them. Baby chickens grow fast, and when their feathers have grown long enough, they go out of doors into a little pen.

Early in May, Papa plants the corn. The horses pull the corn planter up and down the rows. Every little way, three or four kernels of corn are dropped into the row and covered up. After that, the horses are hitched to a thing called a "drag." This completely covers the corn with dirt. Soon the green leaves will come through the ground. It is a pretty sight. The sun and the rain which God sends us, will make it grow, and in October, Papa will hitch the horses to a wagon and go through the field picking the golden ears. The corn is used to feed the farm animals through the winter.

Mamma and I are busy planting the garden. Papa has plowed the ground and worked it until it is nice and smooth. First we take a long piece of string with a stick tied to each end. We put one stick in the ground, unwind the string, and put the other stick in the ground in another place. Then we take a hoe and following the string, we make a trench in which to plant the seeds. We must be careful not to plant the seeds too thickly or they will not grow well. We plant radishes, lettuce, carrots, beets, peas, beans and corn. The tomato seeds are planted in little pots in March, and then the little plants are replanted in the garden. The onions are also partly grown and replanted. We cut potatoes up in pieces, being careful to leave what Mamma calls the "eye," and plant the pieces to make new potatoes grow. What a busy time it is, but I am learning to do many things. It is a good life, as we have lots of good things to eat and lots of fresh air and exercise. Mamma says, "Dorothy, you are growing like a weed! I will soon have to make you some new dresses."

Spring is a beautiful time in Iowa. The grass in the pastures is green. The oats are growing. The trees and bushes are getting their leaves. By the end of May, the lilacs will be blooming. I have never smelled anything so wonderful in my life. On May 30, we pick flowers and take them to the cemetery to put on the graves. I make a special little bouquet to put on Mamma and Papa's little girl's grave. Her name was Clara Mae, and I am the little girl who took her

---

What companionship?   What recreation?

Other children   Wholesome

Kind of work?   Hours.

Helps mother   Reasonable

Is the Child a regular attendant at Church or Sunday School?   Day School?   In what Grade

Irregular   Yes   3

Has Child missed any days at School during past year?   Cause?

Yes, afew, sickness.

Here summarize result of visit.

Dorothy is growing fast and is the picture

of health. She is deeply attached to her foster

parents who idolize her. They have asked our consent

for adoption and I heartily recommend it. Mr. John-

son has just built a fine new barn and next year in-

tends to build a house.

Dorothy is very bright in school. Her

place. School is out now, so I have lots of time to play as well as help Mamma.

In June, we pick strawberries. Mamma makes some round biscuits called "shortcake." We cover them with the fresh strawberries and pour on the thick, rich cream. Mmm!

The Fourth of July is an exciting time. We have a picnic, and then at night we go to the fairgrounds to watch the big fireworks display.

By August, the oats are ready to be harvested. The horses pull a machine called a binder through the field. The binder cuts the stems of "stalks" and binds them into bundles. When all the oats are cut, the bundles are piled into stacks. Later on, they will be hauled into the barnyard and run through a machine called a "threshing" machine. The kernels of oats are funneled into a wagon, hauled to a bin, and unloaded. Later, they are ground into feed for the animals. The golden straw is blown into a pile and later used to make a comfortable bed for the farm animals.

Mamma and I cook a big meal to feed the hungry men each day at dinner time. Things left in the garden must be gathered and put away before the cold weather comes.

Then it is September and school again.

It has been a wonderful summer, and I have learned a lot. Of course, it wasn't all work. I played with my doll, read stories, and went visiting. I spent many happy hours in the swing Papa made for me. I learned that nice poem that Robert Louis Stevenson wrote:

How do you like to go up in a swing,
Up in the air so blue?
Oh, I do think it's the pleasantest thing,
Ever a child can do.

Isn't that nice?

My dog, Spot, and I have fun, too. He loves to try to catch a ball when I throw it. My kitten, Fluffy, is now full grown and sometimes wants to watch for mice rather than play with me.

October is an interesting month. Sometimes it is warm and the sky is a special blue. Then some days are cloudy and cold. The trees put on one last wonderful display — of gold, red and crimson leaves. Everywhere there are piles of orange pumpkins and dark green squash. Jack-o'-lanterns grin at you from porch and fence posts. We have all of these beauties to store in our hearts for the cold winter days ahead.

I was beginning to think that Thanksgiving would never come, but Mamma is already talking about food. Her twin sister and her sister's husband will eat dinner with us if the snow hasn't blocked the roads. Mamma checks her cupboards for sugar, flour, and spices. We won't have turkey, but there is a nice, big chicken waiting to be stuffed and baked to a golden brown. Many of the vegetables we raised in our garden will be on our table on Thanksgiving Day. There will be the butter we have churned ourselves and plenty of thick whipped cream to go on the pumpkin

pie. Mamma will bake some of her delicious bread, and there will be plenty of homemade jam and jelly. Oh, what a feast that will be!

With Thanksgiving over, we will begin to make things for Christmas. Papa says I am not to go into his workshop. I wonder what he is doing there. I know that Mamma is making something after I go to bed. I can hear her sewing machine. She is helping me hem some nice white handkerchiefs. At school, our teacher is helping us make some things to give to our parents. We have woven some mats out of pretty paper for mothers. Our fathers will get a little notebook we have made. I put a picture of a dog on mine. What will I find in my stocking? I hope it is an orange because Christmas is the only time we have oranges. Last Christmas I carried my orange around until Mamma said I must eat it or it would spoil. I didn't want to eat it — it smelled so good.

What a wonderful year it has been. Thank you, Mamma and Papa, for all you have given me, done for me, and taught me.

Chapter VI

Growing Up

Now I am twelve and old enough to belong to a 4-H Club. 4-H stands for Head, Health, Heart and Hands, and we learn many useful things, such as sewing, cooking, canning, raising a garden or an animal, music appreciation, or giving a demonstration. We have fun times, too, and delicious lunches.

Our leader's name is Mrs. Geigel, and she is a very talented lady.

One of my best friends at 4-H is Ella Weber. We like to do the same things and to dress alike. Ella lives on a farm too. She has two brothers and a sister. We are going to do a demonstration at our County Fair. I hope we win first place.

My birth mother has come to Iowa to visit me and my adoptive parents. I am happy to get to see her, but I don't want to go live with her. Mr. and Mrs. Johnson are my papa and mamma now. I like living on a farm. I like my school and my friends. I am bigger than my birth mother. She is only four feet and eleven inches tall. I have been asking about her family, but she won't tell me much. Her mother (my grandmother) died when my mother was small. Her father (my grandfather Tyler) came from England. He bought some land in Florida, but when my mother was a teenager, he sold the land and went back to England. She would not go with him, as she felt he preferred her brother and that he did not love her. She also said the King of England had given my grandfather some kind of honor in return for a favor he had done for the King. After her father left, she got a job taking care of some children. At church she met my father and shortly married him. They became the parents of ten children, of which I was number nine. I had seven brothers, six of whom were older than I was. I had two sisters, too, but they died before I was born, and so I never knew them.

She hasn't told me much about my brothers either. She did tell me that the reason she gave "Buddy," Charles, and me to the New York Children's Aid Society was because three

Dorothy's birth mother

of my older brothers were in military service, so she had no one to help provide for us. She had a heart problem and had to have surgery, too. I'm sure it was a hard decision. Buddy is going back to New York with her. Mrs. Rawson never adopted him, and she wasn't very kind to him. How fortunate I am; my adoptive parents love me very much and are good to me. Tomorrow my birth mother and my brother will be going back to New York. I think it is best. Mamma and Papa have been very gracious, but I am sure they have worried that I would want to leave them. I have been glad to see my birth mother, but they needn't have worried — this is my home now. I can write letters and keep in touch, but I would be a very ungrateful person if I were to leave now. "Good-bye, Mamma and Buddy."

Now I am back in school, and today our teacher, Miss White, told us that we are to write a one hundred and twenty-five word theme on something we enjoy doing. Well, that's easy. What is more enjoyable than going to the County Fair? The rides, the exhibits, the animals, the eating places, and the stands where you can play a game and win a prize are plenty to write about. From the minute you buy your ticket and enter the gate, the excitement builds. The sights and smells are marvelous. When I am out of the car, I hurry to find my friend, and we start the rounds.

Our first stop is at a building called the Floral Hall. In it are all kinds of exhibits — flowers, fruit, vegetables, and home-canned fruits and vegetables. There are jams and jellies, pickles and relishes. There are all kinds of sewing: dresses, aprons, and beautiful embroidered things such as pillowcases, tea towels, tablecloths and dresser scarves. Quilts with all kinds of patterns hang on the walls. There are knit sweaters and afghans and all kinds of crocheted doilies and even some things with tatted trims. Fastened to many of those things there are purple ribbons, which mean "First Prize." Second prize is a red ribbon, and third prize is a white one. Each one who wins a prize gets some money.

On our way to see the animals, we stop to look at the machinery. Farmers love this part of the Fair. They can see all these things that will help them do a better job. Some of the machinery can help them do their work more quickly and easily.

As we move on, we know we are getting near the buildings where the animals are kept. The smells! The sounds! There are pigs, cows, horses, sheep, chickens, and sometimes geese and ducks. What a noise! The pigs grunt, and the cows moo. Sometimes a little lamb says, "Baa-baa. I want my mother." Prizes are given here, too, and proud is the person who gets a purple ribbon. Boys and girls also bring animals and keep them in the 4H building. They compete for prizes, too.

After we have seen all we want to see, we head for the fun and food area. There are hot dog and hamburger stands. At some places you can get a complete meal. Of course, there is popcorn and that amazing, wonderful stuff called "cotton candy." I pull it off the holder, piece by piece, and savor the taste as it melts in my mouth.

I am ready to try one of the rides now. My friend and I discuss which one it will be. Shall we ride the merry-go-round or the Ferris wheel? Maybe we will get to do both as the Fair lasts for five days. Papa says he thinks we can attend more than one day. This will be something to remember for a long time. While we are trying to make up our minds, some other friends come by. We all decide: the Ferris wheel! What a thrilling sensation as we leave the ground and the Ferris wheel starts up, and when we get to the top we can see all over the Fairgrounds — it is almost like flying. We can hear the music from merry-go-round. The people on the ground look like dolls walking around. After the ride, we need some food. We decide on a hot dog with all of the trimmings. We walk around eating it, talking, laughing, and greeting people we know. Everybody goes to the Fair!

There is a building on Fairgrounds called the "Grandstand." There are tiers of seats to sit in and see different programs. In the afternoon, there are different kinds of things. One is horse racing. Men sit in a little cart, which is pulled by a horse. Several horses and carts race around an oval track. Of course, the fastest horse wins. I don't like that part of the Fair very much.

Papa has to go home to feed the animals, but Mamma and I stay at the Fairgrounds. When Papa comes back, we eat at one of the stands. As soon as it gets dark, we find a good place to sit, spread a blanket on the ground, and wait for the fireworks. As the rockets go up in the air and burst into dazzling reds, blues, and greens, I can hear "oohs" and "ahs" all around me. Then the big display comes on — a clown, a train, a waterfall. Then the finale-a wonderful, big red, white and blue American flag. We all stand up and cheer.

Soon the Fair is over, we are back in school, and life gets back into its regular pattern. I am taking piano lessons now. After school I must practice for an hour. My teacher is an older lady. She is very patient with me. She teaches me for one hour, and Mamma pays her fifty cents.

Tonight we are going to a meeting at a neighbor's house. It is called "Farm Bureau." It is an organization that helps farmers with their concerns and problems. We will have a speaker, a business meeting, and then lunch. If the weather is nice, the children will play out of doors. If it is cold, we will have to stay indoors. We have been warned by our parents that we must be quiet. If we aren't, there are liable to be some serious consequences when we get home.

We have been invited by our neighbors, Mr. and Mrs. Capeseius, to come to their home sometime soon to hear a wonderful new invention called a radio. We have to take turns listening because there is no speaker, and we have to use headphones. It is wonderful to hear people many miles away. The radio station is in Pittsburgh, Pennsylvania. The station is called KOKA.

Another fun thing is our neighborhood barn dances. When the haymow is empty and clean and before the new crop of hay comes in from the field, the neighbors gather together for an evening of fun and food. The band may consist of only one fiddler, but the atmosphere is jolly, and we can sing along. Everybody comes! When the babies and small children get sleepy, the pile of coats in the corner makes a good bed. Grandpa and Granddaughter make a cute couple as they glide around the floor. Little boys may be dancing with young ladies — no age requirements here. When everyone has finally run out of breath, lunch is served. The delicious sandwiches, cakes and pies put the final touch on an enjoyable evening, and even the little ones are allowed a few sips of the fragrant coffee.

Being twelve has been so much fun. I am doing well in school. Of course, it is exciting to think that after next year I will be going to high school. I can hardly believe things have turned out so well for me. Although I sometimes wonder what my life would have been like in New York, I am very thankful for what I have. Buddy is old enough now so that he can help our birth mother, and Baby Charles is now a little boy of nine. My memory of him is so very dim, but I hope he has a good home, too. Maybe someday I can find him.

I wonder if there is lots of snow and cold weather in Canada. I guess Charles still lives there. I wish I could see him. I write letters to my brothers and birth mother. Sometimes they send me pictures. I wrote a letter to Miss Comstock when I finished eighth grade. She was so glad that I got good grades and is happy that I got a good home.

Today at school George was teasing me about being adopted, so I told him, "My parents chose me. Your parents had to take what they got." When I told Mamma about it, she said, "That is true, Dorothy, but I don't want you to be rude. It is always better to be kind and polite to people. We should do unto others as we would have others do unto us." Isn't that nice?

Papa is busy building roads. He uses horses to pull the machinery. First he uses a piece of machinery called a scraper to dig ditches. The dirt is then pulled up on the road and a grader smooths it down.

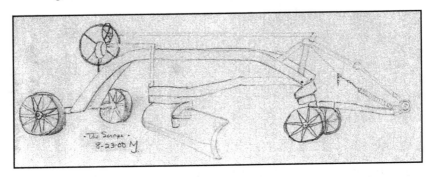

When he is not building roads, he cultivates corn and mows the hay. When the hay is dry, he takes it into rows. He gathers it up, puts it in big piles or stores it in the haymow. This makes good food for the horses and cows in the winter.

Chapter VII

High School and Teaching

This is my first day at Algona High School. I am so afraid I will do something stupid, and the other young people will laugh at me. Some of them have always lived in town and went through all the grades with each other. I'm from a one-room country school. I'm afraid I'll be homesick, too. You see, I've got to stay in town from Monday till Friday afternoon when Papa comes to take me home. I will stay with Mrs. Stewart, an older lady. She cooks my meals, too. I don't much like oatmeal, but I guess I'll get used to it. I take my lunch to school with me. It's too far for me to walk home, eat lunch and get back to school on time.

The high school is a two-story gray brick building with a basement. On two sides are fire escapes. These are big round tubes slanting down from the second floor to the ground. The assembly room on the second floor has doors to the fire escape. There is a little door in each side of the assembly room to get into them. Then we slide down to the ground. (I hope I never have to get into that thing!) The restrooms and gymnasium are in the basement.

First thing in the morning, everyone goes to the assem-

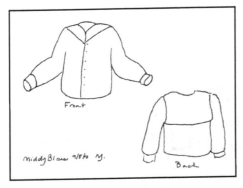

bly room and again after lunch. We change rooms for each class, and each class has a different teacher. Some classes are required; some we are able to choose. Everyone must take gym. We girls wear "middy blouses" and bloomers for gym class.

Of course, high school isn't all lessons and work. Since I live in the country and don't have a car, I can't go to many football or basketball games, but there are always neighborhood parties. Now that I'm old enough to date, that means good times too. My friend, Elsa, wants me to go on a double date with her brother, Charles. We will go in Elsa's friend's

roadster. A roadster is a small car. The back seat opens up, but it has no top so it will be dusty since our roads are gravel. The back seat is sometimes called the "rumble seat." Some people jokingly call it the "mother-in-law" seat.

When winter comes and the snow is on the ground, my friends and I get together for a bobsled ride. There may be a little hand-holding under the horsehair robe that we use to keep warm. The moon shining on the white snow makes it look like a fairy land. The cold crisp air makes us feel alive — we laugh, tell jokes, and sing as the horses pull us along. By the time we reach our host's house, we are famished. The hot cocoa not only warms our tummies, but our hands as well as we hold the hot mugs between our fingers. Before long we have eaten all the delicious cookies Ella's mother made for us. Later, it's time to go home to a warm bed. We have such happy times.

May 23, 1927. Today is my sixteenth birthday, and Mamma is giving me a party. She has taken pink and white crepe paper and gathered it so it looks like ruffles. She then pasted it around the edge of paper plates and put her white dinner plates on top. It is so elegant-looking. I am sure my friends will be impressed. There will be sixteen of us in all — my birthday number. Mamma made a white cake with pink icing. The punch is made with strawberry extract. Strawberries line the edges of the plates. The dining room is decorated with pink and white streamers hung from the center of the room. We will eat, play games, and then I will open my presents. My present from Mamma and Papa is a lovely lavender voile dress with ruffles. Mamma made it for me; it will be my Sunday dress. Oh, my Mamma is so sweet and kind.

Today I got a birthday card from Miss Comstock. She doesn't know much about Charles except that the people who adopted him moved to Canada. They changed his name, too; it is now John S. Craig. Miss Comstock told me that the rest of my family is doing fine and taking care of my mother. Maybe someday my adoptive parents and I can go to New York to visit them.

Mamma's health is not good, so I may not go back to school in September. If she has an operation, I will cook and keep house. She has been so good to me that I can help and go back to school next year. I did go back to school next fall and graduated from high school.

May 1931. In a few days I will graduate from high school. It will not be the same class I started with as Mamma had to have surgery when I was in tenth grade. I stayed home and kept house. She could not do any work for six months. I'm glad I did. My adoptive parents have been very good to me. I have grown up some, too, and I'm sure my grades have been better.

I will be teaching in a one-room country school this fall. I'm excited about that. I remember some of my teachers; they were good examples for me and have influenced my life. I hope I will be a good example and an influence on my students' lives.

This has been a wonderful year. I have been able to enter into more school activities. I love Glee Club as I like music and love to sing. Playing basketball has been fun, too.

Miss Coate, the principal, is such a nice lady. She has taught three generations. She is a strict disciplinarian, but very fair. She was my Latin teacher when I was a freshman. I didn't like Latin; algebra wasn't one of my favorite subjects either. I can see now that both subjects are useful in my life.

I loved our Junior-Senior banquet. It was such fun to dress up. My graduation dress is a lovely white organdy with eyelet trim. My graduation present from Mamma and Papa is a beautiful gold wristwatch with my initials, D.M.J., engraved on the back.

This summer I will help Mamma with her housework and garden and get ready to teach in the fall. I have already signed a contract. The school is twenty miles away from my home, so I will be staying at Uncle Harvey and Aunt Ellen's home during the week. Papa will come for me on Friday afternoon so I can go home for the weekend. Just think, I will be earning seventy dollars a month! Of course, I will pay Uncle Harvey seven dollars a week for room and board. That will leave me some money to put in the bank.

The high school graduate

In the contract I have signed, I promise to "faithfully instruct and impartially govern all pupils…keep daily records and prepare all reports." The United States flag must also be displayed when school is in session and the weather is suitable. I have also promised to take good care of

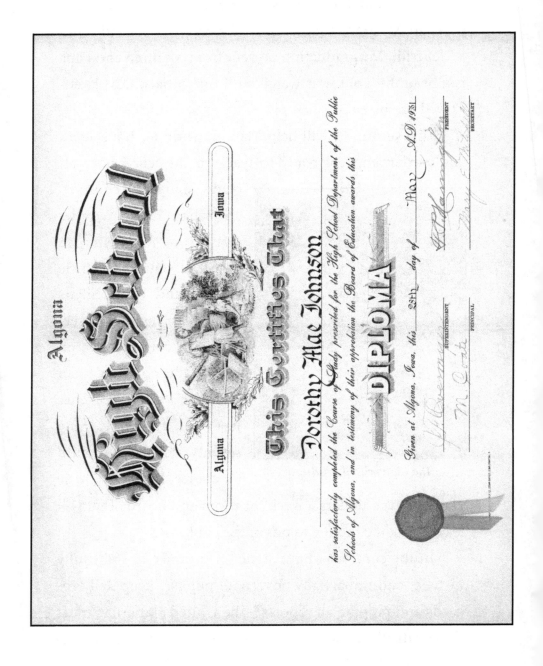

school property.

School will be in session for thirty-six weeks. It is not in my contract, but it is understood by parents and me that I will be a good example. I like to think we need to care about our influence on other people, especially children.

September 5, 1931. This is my first day of teaching. I made a lot of things to make the schoolroom attractive. On the top of the blackboards I put a border of red and gold leaves. I have a vase of goldenrod on my desk. I polished all the desks and hung, a red, yellow and green paper chain over the doorways. I want my students to enjoy school and be eager to be at school every day and enjoy learning.

A One-Room Country School

School days, school days,
Dear old Golden Rule days …

First, let's see what a one-room country school looks like. Probably a square or oblong white wooden building, a belfry with a bell in it. It is usually located on one acre of land. Sometimes it has trees, but often it has no vegetation. Near the back of the building stand two little buildings, one marked "girls," the other marked "boys." Often in the Iowa winters, we had to sweep snow off the seats in the "necessaries" before we could use the building.

Let's look at the inside of the building. Just inside the

door is an entryway (a small hallway) where coats, boots, etc. can be stored. There are two rooms called cloakrooms where we keep our dinner pails and sometimes our wraps, too.

The main room is about twenty-four by forty feet with a raised platform at the far end. The teacher's desk and a recitation bench sit on this platform. On the wall are pull-down maps and blackboards.

Play equipment consists of two swings, a teeter-totter and a bat and ball. The children know lots of games, so recess and noon breaks are spent in active outdoor play unless the weather is very bad. Favorite outdoor games are "Pom-Pom Pull Away" or "Ante I Over." Indoor games are "Button, Button, Who's Got the Button?" and "Animal, Vegetable or Mineral."

In the spring the boys love to catch a snake and chase the girls with it, which may result in disciplinary action. Discipline is not a big problem. The teacher can count on support from the parents. "Teacher" is held in high esteem, and most children want her approval. The teacher has a high standing in the community, and having a school to teach is a sought-after position. Being kept after school is a disgrace since most country children have chores to do at home. Being late causes problems at home. Some children walk two miles, so they are anxious to be on their way when school is dismissed.

Somewhere in the room, usually the center, is a heating

stove which warms a small circle around it. Sometimes it belches forth smoke if the teacher forgets and puts in too many corn cobs at once or if some mischievous boy has climbed on the roof and covered the chimney. Coal and corn cobs are stored in a small building nearby. Either the teacher or one of the big boys carries the fuel to the schoolhouse. The teacher comes very early to school to get the heat started so the children will have a little warmth when they arrive at 9:00 a.m. Sometimes it is so cold the teacher will permit the children to sit on their desks and stomp their feet together to keep warm. Many times the classroom doesn't get warm till noon.

In warm weather, "air conditioning" is windows on both sides of the room opened as far as they will go. A shelf near the cloakroom holds a pail of water with a dipper from which everyone drinks. We place our dinner pails in the cloakroom. Lunch consists of sandwiches, probably homemade bread, a piece of fruit when available, some cookies or a leftover piece of pie, and on Monday a piece of cold chicken left over from Sunday dinner. Sometimes we have one of Mother's homemade pickles or a small jar of home canned fruit, but as hungry as we are, everything tastes good. We may trade another pupil for a piece of her lunch that looks better. Empty syrup cans or lard pails serve as lunch pails.

Our library consists of a big dictionary, a small set of encyclopedias, and a few story books. We have a few good pictures on the walls. Kerosene lamps provide the lights.

Form 52-A8. KLIPTO LOOSE LEAF CO., MASON CITY, IA.

Teacher's Contract for Any District

THIS CONTRACT, Entered into between _Dorothy Mae Johnson_

a legally qualified teacher of _Kossuth_ County, State of Iowa, and

Mike McEnroe President of the Board of Directors of the { School Township / Independent District / Consolidated Independent District

of _Irvington Twp_, County of _Kossuth_, State of Iowa.

WITNESSETH, That in consideration of ($ _75_)

Seventy-five Dollars per school month, the same to be paid at the end of each month, the aforesaid _Dorothy Mae Johnson_ hereby agrees to well and faithfully perform the duties of the teacher in the _No. 5_ District of _Irvington Twp_ to the best of _her_ ability, according to law and the rules legally established for the government thereof, to faithfully instruct and impartially govern all pupils who may attend said school; to keep a daily record and prepare all reports as required by Sections 4339, 4340, Code of Iowa, and to furnish such other data and reports as may be required by the Board of Directors; and furthermore to see that the Flag of Our Country floats over the schoolhouse at all times when school is in session and when weather is suitable therefor, as provided by Section 4253, Code of Iowa, and to exercise due diligence in the preservation of ALL property belonging to the District, such as schoolhouse, furniture, flag, apparatus, and such other property as may reasonably come within the limits of _her_ supervision, for a term of _36_ weeks, commencing on the _5_ day of _September_ 193 _2_.

AND IT IS FURTHER AGREED:

(a) That _s_he is not at this date under contract with any other school district, and that the said Board in entering into this contract, does not violate Section 4229, Code of Iowa.

(b) That _s_he holds a valid certificate which meets the state requirements for approval and will register such certificate with County Superintendent before any part of salary is drawn, as provided by Section 3888, Code of Iowa.

In consideration of said services the said _____ President of the Board in behalf of said District, hereby agrees that the schoolhouse and other buildings shall be kept in good repair and in proper condition for the maintenance of the comfort and health of the teacher and pupils; that the school shall be provided with a suitable flag and flag staff in compliance with School Laws of Iowa; and that said teacher shall be provided with fuel, furniture, school records, apparatus and such other fixtures and supplies as are necessary for the best interests of the school; that the schoolhouse shall be scrubbed and cleaned when necessary, all in compliance with Chapter 213, Code of Iowa; and he further agrees that said teacher shall be paid the sum of ($ _____)

Dollars a month for _____ school months at the end of each month.

Provided: That in case the certificate of said teacher shall be legally revoked, or shall expire during the term of school designated by this contract or that _____ be legally dismissed by the Board of Directors, then said teacher shall not be entitled to compensation after said dismissal, revocation, or expiration of such certificate. Provided, further, that the wages of said teacher for the last month of the school term shall not be paid unless said teacher shall have made the report for the school term as required by law.

IN TESTIMONY WHEREOF, We have hereunto subscribed our names this _4_ day of _April_ 193 _2_

Teacher's School Address _Algona, Ia._ _Dorothy Mae Johnson_, Teacher
_R.F.D. 1_ _M H McEnroe_ President
J A Johnson Subdirector of Dist. No. _5_

NOTE—This contract should be made out in duplicate. One copy should be given to the teacher and one should be filed with the Secretary of the Board. No Board should allow a teacher to commence a term until she has a valid certificate and a written contract properly signed by both parties. All agreements must be in writing.

"Normal Training Certificate"
(equivalent to technical or community college degree)

TEACHER'S MINIMUM SALARY SCALE

Section 4343, Code of Iowa.

The School District cannot legally pay less than the minimum given in the following scale. The teacher cannot accept less. School boards, where possible, should pay their teachers more than the minimum required, according to circumstances and special qualifications. The scale is as follows: Sec. 4341, Code of Iowa.

Graduates of Four Year Course in an Approved College With Iowa State Certificate or Iowa State Diploma.

Minimum Teacher's Wage...$100.00 per Month
Minimum After First Two Years Successful Experience..............$120.00 per Month

Graduates of Two Year Normal Course With Diploma or Equivalent and Who Hold Iowa State Certificate.

Minimum Teacher's Wage...$ 80.00 per Month
Minimum After First Two Years Successful Experience..............$100.00 per Month

Holders of Iowa State Certificates Secured by Examination

Minimum Teacher's Wage...$ 80.00 per Month
Minimum After First Two Years Successful Experience..............$100.00 per Month

High School Normal Training Certificates of Iowa

Minimum Teacher's Wage...$ 65.00 per Month
Minimum After First Year Successful Experience....................$ 75.00 per Month
Minimum After First Two Years Successful Experience..............$ 80.00 per Month

First Grade Uniform County Certificates of Iowa.

Minimum Teacher's Wage...$ 75.00 per Month
Minimum After First Two Years Successful Experience..............$ 80.00 per Month

The preliminary experience required in all cases may be gained on any grade of certificate and on provisional certificates in some cases.

Second Grade Uniform County Certificates of Iowa.

Minimum Teacher's Wage...$ 60.00 per Month
Minimum After First Year Successful Experience....................$ 65.00 per Month

In certain cases Third Grade Certificates may be used. Refer to Code Sec. 4341 for further information.

TEACHERS MUST FURNISH PROOF OF SUCCESSFUL TEACHING EXPERIENCE

The experience called for under this law must be certified to by the County Superintendent before the teacher qualifies for the minimum wage covering such experience.

Pupils range in age from five or six years old to thirteen to fifteen-years old. Four or five rows of desks of various sizes sit in five rows. The smaller children sit in front, nearest the teacher's desk. Each class is called to recite at the recitation bench at the front of the room. One teacher teaches all eight grades in this one room. The same teacher teaches reading, grammar, spelling, history, geography, arithmetic, penmanship, music, health, civics, government, and phonics. The teacher has no supplemental workbooks or materials, only a textbook for each subject. The teacher provides tests, questions to look up and words to define. The teacher writes all these materials in longhand, her only communications tool. Carbon paper is available to make copies if there is more than one pupil needing the test or materials. One example is that of the teacher making up more math questions besides those in the book. If diagramming sentences is the subject, the teacher would add extra ones for practice.

A typical week would go like this:

9:00-9:15 — Opening Exercises (pledge to the flag, sing National Anthem, teacher reads from interesting book)

9:15 -10:15 — Phonics and reading on Mondays, Wednesdays and Fridays; grammar on Tuesdays and Thursdays

10:15-10:30 — Recess

10:30-12:00 — Numbers and arithmetic on Mondays, Wednesdays and Fridays; history or geography on Tuesdays and Thursdays (with periods of recitation of ten to fifteen minutes)

12:00-1:00 — Lunch and Recess

1:00-2:15 — Repeat reading program on Mondays, Wednesdays and Fridays; health on Tuesdays and Thursdays

2:15-2:30 — Recess

2:30-3:50 — Civics and government on Mondays, Wednesdays and Fridays; penmanship or music on Tuesdays and Thursdays

3:50-4:00 — Cleanup and assignments

Once a student completes her work, she may get a book from the library, draw pictures on the blackboard, or make something from construction paper. Older pupils like to help younger ones, and this is a great help to the teacher, too. Extracurricular activities include two programs a year and a basket or pie social.

Now, about the teacher. She is eighteen or nineteen years old and a graduate from Normal I course in high school. Salary is seventy five dollars a month. She applies to the local district trustee for the job. If she marries, she loses her job. She learns to get along with all age groups. She can't teach by words, but by example. Some of the good things about the job are that the teacher has the cooperation of parents and discipline is easy. The pupils are ready to take on adult responsibilities. In later years it is wonderful to see those who succeeded in life. Teaching and learning do not depend on buildings, equipment and materials, but on the quality of the teacher.

One of my students, Rachel P., made me proud. In my second year of teaching, Rachel won the Kossuth County spelling bee. I took her ninety miles to Des Moines to the Iowa State Competition. Teaching has been a joy for me, but soon I will go on to a new life.

Dorothy (far right) and her students

Chapter VIII

Marriage and Family

I won't be teaching school anymore. A fine young man has asked me to be his wife and I said, "Yes." Young ladies who get married can no longer teach country school. Besides, my husband-to-be will not want me to work.

I want to tell you a sweet story; I have named it "The Little House that Love Bought."

It was a cute little house painted robin's egg blue with white trim. It sat on a small lot. Two big oak trees grew by the sidewalk in front of it, and the lawn sloped to the side street. A big windowed porch covered the front. At the back was a small garden plot and a garage. Each side of the house

Dorothy and Irving

had a bay window. The top window was divided into diamond-shaped pieces. These had many corners to clean out at window washing time. The living room stretched the entire width of the house with a fireplace at one end. Behind this was the dining room on the right. A plate rail stretched around two sides. On the left was a bedroom with a bay window. The large kitchen was at the back of the house. Opposite the kitchen was a second bedroom and the bathroom. The lower level was the basement with the furnace, laundry and workshop.

It had belonged to Papa's parents. They had both passed away, and it was now up for sale. Irving and I were engaged, but we had not yet decided where we would live. I had told him I would like to live there. Of course, I didn't think it was possible to buy this little house.

But love finds a way. Ir-

Certificate of Marriage

STATE OF IOWA, *Kossuth* COUNTY

THIS IS TO CERTIFY, that on the 23 day of *August* A. D. 1933 at *Algona, Iowa* in said County according to and by authority of law, I duly

Joined in Marriage

Irving L. Weh

and

Dorothy M. Johnson

Given under my hand the 23 day of *August* A. D. 1933

Marriage solemnized in the presence of

Lucile Black

Lyle Raney

Rev. Arthur D. Hueser

Algona Iowa.

ving wanted to please me, and please me he did! He come on the next date and announced, "I bought your little house today." Wow, there were hugs and kisses that day!

On August 23, 1933, Irving and I were married. It was a very simple ceremony at the parsonage. I wore a pink and blue dimity dress and a large floppy hat, quite stylish! Lucille Black was my maid of honor and Lyle Raney was Irving's best man. We had four guests: Mamma and Papa, Aunt Clara and Cousin Russell.

Our honeymoon was a trip to the World's Fair in Chicago. We came back to Iowa to stay with my parents for a few days until the little house was cleaned and ready. Next came the "charivari."

Neighbors of newlyweds planned this celebration. They hoped to catch the unsuspecting couple at home in the evening. The crowd would gather with all the noisemakers they could find. Surrounding the house, they banged, rang, shouted, etc. until the newlyweds appeared and promised them a party in the near future. Having been part of similar occasions, we were prepared, learned that a crowd was coming, and slipped away to hide in

Charivari for Newlyweds-
One hundred relatives, neighbors, and other friends gathered at Mr. and Mrs. J. A. Johnson's, Rich Point, last week Wednesday night to charivari Mr. and Mrs. Irving Urch. The latter is a daughter of the Johnsons. THe Urches saw the crowd coming and slipped out a back door. A thorough search failed to locate them, but they reappeared from a cornfield and were caught later by a rear guard after most of the crowd had ostensibly gone away. The crowd then came back but broke up when the newlyweds promised an ice cream feast later.

a nearby cornfield. Of course, the crowd was disappoint-
ed and soon left, (so we thought). What sneaky friends
— while all the cars drove away, some boys hid in a ditch.
When we came back to the house, these fellows surrounded
it. We were trapped! When the rest of the crowd came back,
we succumbed gracefully and promised an ice cream party
soon. We kept our promise.

Mamma would have said, "Pride goeth before a fall,"
which proved to be true of my first Thanksgiving as a bride.

Irving and I invited his two aunts, their husbands and
families to eat Thanksgiving dinner with us. Of course, I
wanted everything to be perfect. The house was cleaned,
scoured and polished to such a perfection that we could
hardly breathe. If we did, we might disturb the arrange-
ments or find a spot of dust. The dining room table was covered with a cutwork embroidered tablecloth, a wedding gift
from my birth mother. Twelve places were set with matching china, five pieces of silverware and crystal goblets. The
tablecloth and napkins were starched and ironed. The napkins were folded perfectly with edges matching.

The menu was a work of art. The turkey looked like the
picture in the cookbook. The vegetables and dressing were
hot and ready to serve in the proper bowls, and servers were
at hand.

After a prayer of thanks, the guests sat at their places with napkins on their laps. As Irving started passing the
bowls and platters of food, the guests seemed to be distract-

ed by something at their feet. What was wrong here? The starched napkins were so stiff that they slid from everyone's lap. As Mamma said, "Pride … ."

Everyone had a good laugh about Dorothy's slippery napkins. For years family members repeated the story at family gatherings.

Two years later I was Mamma to little Albert, named after his paternal grandfather. He was a healthy baby, walking and talking when he was a year old. His grandparents loved him and often took him home to spend the night.

December 1937. Irving's uncle bought a farm in Minnesota. He wants us to move there and farm it. That will mean leaving my little honeymoon house and moving into a house that has no running water, no furnace, and no bathroom. We will have to rent our house in Algona. It was a big decision to make. Of course, we have to make a lot of decisions in a lifetime. This will take a lot of thought and prayer.

Irving would like to try it. He has worked in a grocery store so many years. He started working there when he was still young, and that was where I met him. We think it would improve his health if he could work out-of-doors.

March 1938. The decision is made, and we moved into the little five-room house on the Minnesota farm. Caring and milking fourteen dairy cows will be a new experience for us. It will be a lot of work, but we will be only half a mile away from Irving's uncle and mother. They will be glad to help and advise us.

The weather is still cold in March, but there is a lot to be done. The men will go to auctions to buy machinery and other things we will need. Of course, the cows must be fed every day, the barn cleaned, and milking done every morning and evening. The milk must be separated from the cream and put in a cool place until it is sold and taken to the cheese factory. My job is to keep the milk pails, the separator and the milk cans clean. That is very important.

As spring comes on, we begin to plan for planting. Oats are the first crop we plant, then corn and soybeans. The work will be similar to that on an Iowa farm when I was a girl. Of course, now I will have more responsibilities. There will be baby chickens to care for, and Irving will have baby pigs and calves to care for.

I wonder if Charles lives on a farm. He will now be a man in his twenties. A lot of Canada is farm country. Maybe he works with his adoptive father, who is a railroad man.

Albert loves the farm. He likes to pretend he is a farmer and is helping his father. He has a pair of overalls, an overall jacket, and a cap to match. He was very frightened the other day. He has a bright red handkerchief, which he wears in his jacket pocket. As he was helping gather eggs, a big old rooster jumped up and pulled the handkerchief right out of his pocket. When the weather gets warm, we will make him a sandbox to play in. He has a little red wagon to haul things around and a tricycle to ride.

Irving is busy making a way to run water into the house,

so we won't have to carry it. By drilling a hole in the cellar wall and connecting a pipe to the well, we will have running water in the house. That is such a big help.

The men are also busy cutting trees in the wood. They will bring the wood home and cut it into firewood. In Minnesota we burn wood in our cook stoves instead of coal. Winter is a busy time on the farm. When spring comes, we will be busy planting crops and gardens and taking care of baby chickens, pigs and calves.

Summer

Winter is over at last and farmers are busy cultivating corn and making hay. In late July we will harvest the oats. When the bundles of oats are run through the threshing machine, great piles of golden straw are stacked. In winter this straw is used to make clean, warm beds for the farm animals.

When we take a day off, we go fishing or swimming in a nearby lake. Minnesota is "The Land of Ten Thousand

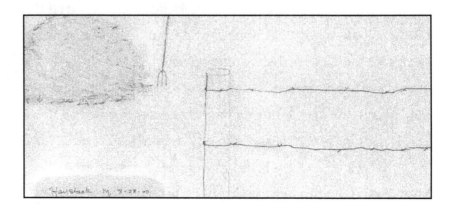

Lakes." Often on Sundays after church and Sunday School, we gather for a family picnic. Golden fried chicken, big bowls of potato salad and baked beans disappear in a hurry. We add juicy pickles which Grandma made from the cucumbers grown in her garden. And, oh, the pies and cakes — what could be better, especially if someone brings home-made ice cream.

The men play ball while the women exchange recipes or talk about the children's needs. Small cousins chase each other shouting at the tops of their voices. They are so full of life they can hardly contain themselves. What a happy time.

Every day is full, and by March 1939, Albert has a sister Jo an, and in 1943 little sister Beverly has joined the family.

Both Jo an and Beverly were born at home. The hospital was twenty miles away, and in March and December the snow may be deep. It was easier for the doctor to come to the farm. So he did, though it meant driving through the fields and over snow banks. We had a hired girl for a few weeks to help with the housework and the new baby. Evelyn was good help, but she had two failings. She poured the oatmeal flakes into the boiling water too rapidly, making lumpy oatmeal. She always put too much wood in the cook stove, got the oven too hot and had to let it cool before she could bake the bread. But those were happy times, and there was lots of laughter in the little house in Minnesota.

The years went by fast and before I knew it, it was Albert's first day at the little schoolhouse a mile away.

Today, June 25, 1943, Mamma died. She had not been well, but this was unexpected. She was propped up in her bed and just went to sleep. I am so glad she didn't suffer. She was such a good Mamma to me and loved me so much. I am very fortunate to have had two good mothers who loved me and wanted the best for me.

Now we have another big decision to make. Papa wants us to move back to Iowa. (He still lives on the farm where I grew up.) We can live on the farm, and he will live with us. That way we can make a home for him. We move back to Iowa and start another era in our lives.

Albert had gone to live with his grandfather and start school. By spring we were settled in and busy with farm work. Again there were baby chickens to care for and a garden to be tilled. Farm life is busy, and it is a wonderful place to live and grow up.

When baby Donald joined the family in 1945, we felt our life was complete — two fine healthy boys and two sweet girls to care for and raise.

Busy years followed busy years with school and projects on the farm. They also did jobs of various kinds to earn spending money.

For entertainment, there were slumber parties and skating parties. A horse and bicycles furnished many happy hours of fun and exercise.

Year passed quickly with graduations from kindergarten, elementary school and high school. Then it was time for college. That meant a new phase of life for me. I was now the mother of a college student. My first-born chose Bob Jones University in Greenville, South Carolina, and left Iowa to go there. Two years later, Irving and I decided we would like the other three children to attend the same school. We rented the farm and moved to South Carolina.

We spent summers in Iowa. The children graduated from college; they married, and Donald was in military service. Irving and I were again alone. Over the next few years we became grandparents. That's exciting!

Dorothy and Irving Urch with their children

Chapter IX

Older Years

People often think and feel that growing older means there is no more they can do, and that they are no longer useful. My husband, Irving, and I did not find that to be true. We worked at Miracle Hill, Greenville, South Carolina's Rescue Mission's home for children, at a Christian Day School, our church camp, and at a camp in Canada for Indian children.

We had a little place on Lake Hartwell. There we spent many happy hours boating, fishing, swimming and entertaining. Our grandchildren loved to be there and could hardly wait for the weather and the water to be warm enough for swimming and water-skiing.

Helping at Miracle Hill Children's Home was very rewarding. I could understand how the children felt. Because of conditions in the home, it was best for the children to be away for a time. Irving and I could be substitute Grandma and Grandpa. Having grandparents was something I missed as a child.

Planning and cooking hot lunch for the Christian Day School gave me pleasure while Irving saw that the school buses were in good shape. He took pride in fixing things that needed repair. I worked two years in the school library, another task that gave me pleasure.

Cooking at a camp was one of the things Irving and I loved most to do. Our church had a camp in the South Carolina mountains. It is a challenge to plan for all the meals for five days, get the supplies together and cook all this food for the young people. With the nearest store being forty miles away, there was not room for mistakes.

Canada is a beautiful country. Manitoba has many lakes. As you travel, you will see deer and occasionally a bear. The lakes abound in geese, ducks, and loons. The call of the loon is a weird sound and can make cold chills go up your spine, especially if you hear one after dark.

The brown-skinned Indian children are very loving. They rewarded us with their love and their wonder that someone cared enough for them to travel many miles to cook for them.

Irving and I both loved to travel, and our little camper made a substitute home. It's a good idea to take plenty of

warm bed covers for the Canada trip, nights can be pretty cold, even in July.

We did not

spend all our time working. We took two Caribbean cruises. It was wonderful to have someone else do the work for our enjoyment. It was a joy to sail on God's beautiful ocean and to see other people and countries.

Sometimes I thought about Charles, where he was living, and if he was enjoying the good things of life. I wondered if he had grandchildren. Did he know about his birth family? Would he like to meet us?

Irving and I enjoyed gardening and planting flowers. We enjoyed keeping our little house clean and painted. Church, family and friends were a big part of our lives.

Eventually Irving's failing health caused us to spend more time at home. We learned to love and appreciate each other very much. It was a sad day for me when he died.

Living alone was too hard for me. In November 1993, I moved into a retirement home. I soon had many new friends and kept busy making quilts and doing all kinds of crafts.

In 1997 while attending a health class, I learned that I had probably gone from New York to Iowa on an Orphan Train.

A trip to Algona, Iowa, and a visit to the County Historical Society produced a newspaper article that confirmed this.

I was now on a new adventure. With my family's help, I began to recall names and places and incidents from my childhood. In June 1999, my two daughters and I met with the archivist of the New York Children's Aid Society. Searching old records verified my findings and gave us more information. In May 2000, I attended an Orphan Train reunion in New York City, hosted by the New York Children's Aid Society.

I now tell my story to schools, civic organizations, and groups of senior citizens. I have been very blessed, and I now know: "Why."

Dorothy, center, with other Orphan Train riders at reunion in NYC

Chapter X

The Happy Ending

Do you remember how I told you at the beginning of my story about my baby brother, Charles? The years went by, and I heard no more about him. I knew his name had been changed from Charles Brooks to John Craig. The family had moved to Ontario, Canada. I met with and corresponded with my birth mother and the rest of my brothers several times over the years. I wanted more and more to know if Charles was living and where. My family helped me investigate using the Internet. My daughter found him using Social Security records.

Charles, found at last

Charles passed away twenty-two years ago, but we found his widow and his four sons. We had a joyful reunion in July 1999.

Do you like a happy ending? I do. Of course, there is always "I wish." But we can't expect things to be perfect, and

The John Craig (Charles Brooks) family

we need to be grateful for what we have.

Dear (Charles) John, Miss Comstock was right. Mr. and Mrs. Craig took good care of you. They gave you a good home and a good education. You grew up to be a fine young man. You were a hard worker. You served your country well in the army. You were a good husband and father.

Why God planned it so, I don't need to know. I had

two loving families, my birth mother and brothers, and my adoptive parents. I had a wonderful husband. I have a fine family. I have never wanted for anything, have never been cold or hungry. I have a host of friends, and most of all, a place prepared for me by a loving Savior.

Now that I am finally remembering and learning about Reverend Brace and Miss Comstock, I wish I could see them now in person. And, Miss Comstock, how I wish I could have gone to her, put my arms around her and thanked her for finding such a good home for me. What love and compassion Reverend Brace and his agents had for the poor little "Orphan Train Riders."

Yes, there really was a Miss Comstock.

Yes, there was a baby brother Charles.

Problems today are much the same. Troubles come and for different reasons families separate. The loss of a job, disagreements, abuse of alcohol and drugs separate children from parents. Hearts ache the same as they did eighty years ago. Parents must decide the best for their children, and sometimes separation is the only solution.

How did my mother feel when she released me to the New York City Children's Aid Society? I'm sure it almost broke her heart. She probably shed many tears and spent many sleepless nights wondering if she had done the right thing. It must have been hard, too, to visit me later and have to leave me again. I am sure she was very happy to see that I had a good home and loving adoptive parents.

To My Dear Young Friends

Yes, I can,
I know I must,
I'll pray and try,
And learn to trust.

I'm glad I'm me,
God made me so,
I'll study hard,
I'll work and grow.

I'll do my best,
Just wait and see,
Cause then you
Will be proud of me.

To My Dear Readers

Why God planned it so,
Well, now I know:
He gave me what was best for me.
His plan I did not need to see.

I hope you have enjoyed my story. It is really mine. I was born in New York, May 23, 1911. I was number nine of ten children. Because of the economy and my father's death in 1916, my mother could no longer care for her three youngest children. To keep us from having to live in an orphanage, she released us to the New York Children's Aid Society. Baby Charles was adopted by a couple living in Kansas. They changed his name to John and shortly moved to Canada, and we lost contact with him.

Buddy (Albert) and I were sent to Iowa. I was adopted by a fine couple, Mr. and Mrs. Johnson. Buddy went back to New York in 1923. I really did teach in a one-room country school. I married a fine man by the name of Irving Urch. We had four children. Five summers we traveled to Canada and worked in a camp for Indian children.

Dear Reader, I want you to see that obstacles can be overcome. You can grow up to be what you want to be. Being adopted is to be chosen. There are many loving, caring people in the world. God bless you.

Epilogue

Names, ideas, facts, revelations, inspirations often come to us from the most unexpected sources.

The name Miss Comstock, the New York Children's Aid Society, a baby brother named Charles were some of the names that have often come to mind without any real basis for doing so.

But there really was a New York Children's Aid Society, founding by Charles Loring Brace, which sent 150,000 children on Orphan Trains from New York and placed them in homes in the Midwest.

There also was a flesh-and-blood Miss Comstock, who taught at Brace Farm School until 1911. Then she worked for the immigration department of the New York Children's Aid Society. She stayed with the New York Children's Aid Society for forty-three years.

And there was a baby brother named Charles, who was adopted by a couple living in Kansas. They later moved to Canada.

To sum it all up, my greatest desire is that all of my family will be saved, and that we will have a wonderful reunion in that glorious place where there are no partings and our Heavenly Father will be watching over us all.

I want them to have good marriages, love and respect, a family who will love them and care for them when they are older — as mine does.

Riding an Orphan Train and being placed in a new home all worked for my good. Had I remained in New York, I might never have been saved or had the good husband I had.

Now I am a child again — this time traveling Home to my Heavenly Father.

Acknowledgments

It would be impossible for me to name all who have helped me. A suggestion, a word of encouragement, a show of interest has helped me search and record all that now constitutes my little book. Pat Stewart's suggestion that I might have been on an Orphan Train, and my family's prodding my memory was the beginning. People who have heard my story and asked, "Why don't you write a book?" have given me the energy to complete the task.

My great-grandson Joshua Medlin's artistic ability has certainly added a wonderful touch. All the children who have listened to my story showed me the reason for putting down my story in writing.

Thanks to my publisher, Donald Urch, who put it all together in a form that makes it accessible to all.

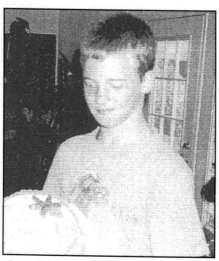

Grandson and artist Joshua Medlin

About the Author

Dorothy Urch was eighty-five years old when she attended a Health-Wise class in Greenville, South Carolina. When she shared with the group that she had been born in New York and adopted in Algona, Iowa, she learned she might have been an Orphan Train rider. Doro-thy had never heard of Orphan Train riders and had no recollection of her trip to Iowa. But because of this, she began to do research into her life.

She was the ninth of ten children. Two sisters died before she was born in 1911. Of the surviving children, three were placed for adoption, one younger than she and one older. Her older brother was also sent to Algona, Iowa. The younger brother was adopted in Kansas and then moved to Canada. Through her research she was able to make contact with the families of all of her siblings except for the child who moved to Canada. She saw her birth mother again in 1923 when she came to visit her in Iowa. Dorothy traveled to White Plains, New York, around 1931 to visit her mother. She never learned any more about her biological father, who died when she was very young.

Dorothy's adoptive parents in Algona were loving parents. Dorothy came into their lives after the death of their thirteen-month-old daughter. She became their daughter in every way. She had in her possession photos of herself and her new parents.

After completing her schooling, Dorothy became a teacher in a one-room schoolhouse. Within two years she married and raised four children. She lived in both Iowa and Minnesota. She ended up in South Carolina because her oldest son chose to attend Bob Jones University in Greenville. He enjoyed it so much that the entire family moved there, and all her children wound up attending Bob Jones.

After discovering more about her roots, Dorothy devoted her time and energy, for as long as she was able, to promoting the work of the Orphan Train Heritage Society of America. Because she shared her story in schools and with civic organizations, the Orphan Train era will long be remembered as a part of American history.

Dorothy Urch died in 2007.

Dorothy's children had the following comments about how being one of the estimated two to three million descendants of orphan train riders has affected them:

At the age of eight, this Iowa farm girl was excited
to find out she had uncles, aunts, and cousins she

had never met, and to get to travel to New York City to get acquainted with them. In my teen years, I realized what a Godly woman my mother was, and I began to understand how emotionally painful the separation from her family and adjustment to a new family was for her. When we finally located her brother's family, my mother was in her mid-eighties, and it was the best family reunion I ever attended! She spent the rest of the years of her life telling her story to school children and church and civic groups, and writing her story in a book titled Charles Found at Last. *I feel so blessed to call her Mom!*

Jo an Urch Boehm, daughter

My mother's Orphan Train story has been and will continue to be an inspiration and influence on the lives of children, adults and seniors as long as the story is read, told and seen.

Don Urch, son

Being introduced to the "placing out" of many children, including my mother, helped me to better understand her as a person and many of her "ways" of doing things.

Bev Urch Cantrell, daughter